Copyright © 2019 by simply rita

All rights reserved. No part of this publication may be reproduced, distributed, or transmitted in any form or by any means, including photocopying, recording, or other electronic or mechanical methods, without the prior written permission of the publisher, except in the case of brief quotations embodied in critical reviews and certain other noncommercial uses permitted by copyright law. For permission requests, write to the publisher, addressed "Attention: Permissions Coordinator," at the address below.

White Boots 101 Writing Services LLC
whiteboots101writingservicesllc.com

Ordering Information:
Quantity sales. Special discounts are available on quantity purchases by corporations, associations, and others. For details, contact the publisher at the website above.
Orders by U.S. trade bookstores and wholesalers.

Printed in the United States of America

Table of Contents

2. Table of Content
3. Thank You
4. Poems for The Soul
5. My Nothing
6. You
7. The Stars
8. Whiskers
9. F.A.M.L.Y.
10. This Thing
11. Tattered
12. When Searching
13. The Simple Things
14. In Love
15. Weird
16. Overtime
17. Unmask
18. This Man
19. Sometimes
20. Ever
21. The Tears of Christ
22. Weight
23. Love, Love, Love
24. A Little Prayer
25. Deepest
26. My Love
27. Oops
28. It's Raining
29. I'm Fashioned
30. If Good
31. Love For You
32. Even
33. Mind
34. If I Could Change
35. Humbled
36. It's Yours
37. Memory
38. Gentle
39. His Grace
40. There Are Moments
41. A Whisper
42. It's Hard
43. Do You Suppose?
44. Behind the Doors
45. I Know it's Hard
46. Color Blind
47. Before
48. All I Know
49. A Covered Soul
50. Intro to Greeting Card
51. Save a Spot
52. Another Year
53. Graduation Day
54. It Took A While

THANK YOU

I sincerely thank you for your purchase of my book, "Poems for the Soul." I pray that you laugh, fall in love, be inspired, and above all, see the love of Christ in this body of work. I believe my calling is to lift readers up with my gift of poetry. Truly everyone has a calling and it's his or her responsibility to use that gift to encourage others and be a blessing to the household of faith.

As in my past books, I've shared my inner child, my silly side, this hopeless romantic heart, and my deep relationship with God. I write about the blessings of God and the strength we have through Him in trying times. From this book I pray that you will find hope when things are not at their best.

There are rhyming poems, blank verse poems, poems on memory loss, weight gain, and all the things we tend to deal with in life. From them I pray that you find love, enlightenment, hope, and an overall felling of peace from each poem you read.

All work is newly written and/or written some time ago, but never published. I've also included five (5) poems from my up and coming greeting card line. I encourage you to follow your heart, your passion, your dream, whatever it is you feel God has given you to do. When you operate in the gift that you've been given, you will find a peace, rest, and love that can only be experienced when doing what you are called to do.

Write, sing, dance, draw, preach, run for political office, if it's continually in your dreams and on your heart, then chances are, it's your calling and it's time for you to answer the phone. Until my next book, calendar, t-shirt, greeting card project, children stories, please enjoy,

"Poems for the Soul."

simply rita

POEMS FOR THE SOUL

It's time to write for you again
To fans it is my goal
To rhyme for you a line or two
And dare to pierce your soul

For those of you who are anew
I pray that you will find
A calming source, a gentle force
To ease your racing mind

I am the poet on the scene
Continuing the charge
Of lifting you out of your blue
The shoes I fill are large

That Shakespeare from the days of old
Oh, Maya you are here
The poets great they do await
To write a message clear

To love a love as Juliet
Did love her Romeo
Through crying eyes, do dare to rise
For Maya told you so

And what of me what can I say
What message I for you
You are the reason that I write
My passion it is true

It's time to write for you again
Therefore it is my goal
To rise you up, to lift you up
With "Poems for the Soul."

MY NOTHING

My nothing for your everything
My minor for your more
My lesser for your greater than
In this I am secure

My weakness shows your strongest strength
My failures show your rise
My mountain is a chore for me
Until I see your eyes

Like coal they burn forever bright
And yet I'm not consumed
They chisel down into a hill
While I smell like perfume

From there a dust and then it's gone
No more to bother me
How useless was my worried mind
But priceless peace to see

There's nothing that can hinder you
There's something that you bear
I'm guessing I will never know
I'm only glad you care

Perhaps that's why you say to us
Lean not to understand
Your ways are far beyond the mind
And so much more than man

My nothing for your everything
I'll gladly make the trade
The lesser me, but greater you
That's how my calm is made

YOU

I love you

Not only because of who you are, but also for what you are, and that is a VERY big part of me.

I need you

Not because I cannot obtain without you, but because I'd rather not obtain ANYTHING without you.

I think of you

Not only because you're worth thinking about, but because it brings me JOY to think about you.

And I PRAY for you

For your needs
For your wants
And for EVERYTHING pertaining to you

I LOVE YOU

THE STARS

If I could bring the stars to you
And place beside your eyes
Brighter still your baby brown
So back into the skies

And if the sun would dare to say
It's warmer than your heart
The contest it would surely lose
And this is just the start

Your love is greater, better than
The best I've ever known
And just when we have reached our
peak More love from you is shown

There never seems to be a lack
Of love from you to me
The oceans wide and mountains high
Are small and what I see

The elements surrounding us
The couples in our space
Are puzzled by the greatest love
That shows upon our face

The bluest skies or moon per say
Are over shadowed still
And though they try they can't comply
Together as we kneel

A thank you to our Lord above
For happy we both are
The sky, the moon, are both from you
You are the brightest star

WHISKERS

Whiskers, whiskers, on my chin How
dare you grow on me
I tweeze and tweeze, but there you
are For all the world to see

A stubble here a stubble there
More hair across my lips
My razor broke and clippers too
But sasquatch has some tips

He tells me to embrace myself
Or better make a charge
For he has made a living, long
With bigfoot still at large

But I refuse to lose my looks
When looking at my face
With rosy lips and cozy cheeks
All hair to be erased

No hair atop my glossy lips
No whiskers on my arms
My legs are shaved from high to low
No need to be alarmed

I have the longest, thickest, hair
So growing from my head Cascading
down onto my back
And when I rise from bed

Oh what, oh no, where has it gone?
My hair where can it be?
An Esthetician played a trick
Now whiskers cover me

F.A.M.I.L.Y. CREED

We're **F**ormed by His creation
Anointed to withstand
And **M**oved to celebration
Instructed with His hand
Thus **L**ove is no Frustration
When **Y**ielding to His plan

Family
Our Calling
Our Creed

THIS THING

I may not be a scholar known
For facts or wisdom wide
I may not read a lot of books
But this I have inside

I have a gift to comfort you
Some words of coziness
A thought to lift you very high
To make you feel your best

So simple as I strike the keys
To form a verse or two
In moments I have entered in
To chase away your blue

A singer sings angelically
The best I've ever heard
Some dancers dance across a stage
Some preachers preach the word

Though simple is the thing I have
I'm grateful for the gift
Created different you and I
Together when we mix

We meet a need and touch a soul
We make a better place
We brighten up a darken world
We show the Savior's face

So simple is my calling true
But comfort it will bring
A scholar no, a master yes
I'm gifted in this thing

TATTERED

Tattered to a battered state
I search the scriptures deep
By turning pages day and night
And when I start to sleep

I think upon the lessons learned
The message from the Lord
Directions how to daily live
And be in one accord

I flip the pages back and forth
In morning when I wake
I read my bible as a meal
It serves me like a plate

Some meat to make me very strong
Some veggies for my mind
Dessert of peace for me to keep
Oh daily I do dine

I never skip or waste His food
Nutrition for my soul
The bread of life that I may live
And be in His control

That's why it looks as if it's torn
This bible that I read
But I am as the greatest quilt
I'm sown cause I believe

Not tattered and not battered but
I'm molded by His book
And you will be the same as me
If you should take a look

WHEN SEARCHING

When searching for that perfect one
That endless kind of love
Well have you ever raised your eyes
And looked to Him above

At night when you are all alone
Your heart so in despair
Your mind is shouting loud and clear
"You have no one to care."

It is a trick a dirty trick
That Devil's on the prowl
A lion roaring with a lie
His speech forever foul

Well that is when you use your voice
Respond with words of truth
"My God is here, He loves me dear.
He's held me since my youth."

Your heart will start to feel a warmth
Your mind will be at peace
Your spirit it will overflow
And love will be released

The presence of the Holy one
Will fill your darken room
Then light will shine so pure and bright
To chase away your gloom

When searching for that special one
Remember this is true
You're not alone, so don't despair
He's near and He loves you

THE SIMPLE THINGS

A walk in the park in the daylight or dark
THE SIMPLE THINGS

A hand in my hand when I sit, or I stand
THE SIMPLE THINGS

A smile on my face that is wider than space
THE SIMPLE THINGS

The beat in my heart 'til death do we part
THE SIMLPE THINGS

Oh, how I love

THE SIMPLE THINGS

IN LOVE

Have you ever been in love?
I mean that falling kind
The thing that overtakes your soul
Your body and your mind

And have you ever fallen deep?
So deep you cannot speak
You cannot utter any words
Your knees forever weak

Well I have been in such a state
Some thirty years ago
I saw a walking, beating heart
And him I had to know

I looked into the brownest eyes
I've ever seen before
They opened up his inner soul
And showed me even more

A gentleness the sweetest bliss
A need to have a love
And so he looked up to the skies
And prayed to God above

Thus to my glee my fantasy
Became a vision true
And on my day, my wedding day
I proudly said, "I do!"

Oh have you ever been in love?
One day your dream will come
And you will be forever blessed
When you behold the one

WEIRD

I want to speak a simple truth
The secret how I feared
One day the world would come to know
That I am really weird

I simply laugh at everything
I smile when I am sleep
I still believe in unicorns
With love my fall is deep

I take a rope and jump around
In circles I do run
I chase myself around the room
And just before I'm done

I take the mirror off the wall
And place it in my lap
I conversate 'til very late
Not stopping for a nap

As if that was the strangest thing
It's stranger even more
I fight with pillows on the couch
Then roll onto the floor

But maybe if the world would try
To be the same as me
Then love would surely conquer hate
Look through my eyes to see

That weird is not a scary state
In fact I think I'm right
So try to be as weird as me
All day and through the night

OVERTIME

I like a little overtime
To pay a bill or two
The forty plus may be a must
I know it to be true

But sixty on and maybe more
Has beaten every nerve
While aching pains from head to toe
Is more than I deserve

I haven't seen my lover true
I haven't seen my kids
I'm pulling straws to get some time
But rarely win the bid

And then there are the noisy ones
Who say that I complain
That working is a blessing thus
At work I should remain

Yes grateful is my state of mind
I'm glad to have a check
But family is first to me
And home I will not wreck

I will not cut my time with God
In Him I have my health
In Him I have my everything
In Him I find my wealth

I'd rather cut my hours down
So forty here I come
A peace of mind and loving time
With space to have some fun

UNMASK

Unmask is what I want to do
This smile across my face
It's there to hide the pain inside
If you could see this place

You'd see a path I walk alone
At least that's how I feel
You'd hear the whispers screaming loud
"Your heart, it will not heal."

You'd also see the hidden scars
Beneath the sleeves I wear
The cutting that I've done to me
Alas, the fear I bear

Depression is my way of life
Anxiety is more
Bipolar is not far behind
But what I'm looking for?

I'm searching for a friend of friends
Someone to pray for me
My strength when weakness is at hand
My eyes when I can't see

I want a love not of the earth
A love that is from Christ
A love that stretches east to west
Forever would be nice

Unmask is what I've done today
My heart has now the space
To feel a peace I've rarely known
Lord thank you for your grace

THIS MAN

Who is this Man? This Bread of life
This lover of my soul
Who dare to take away my pain?
Who dare to make me whole?

Why pay this price in sacrifice?
Why lay you down for me?
I'd like to say I understand
Alas, I do not see

But I will not prolong my thoughts
Of whys, of when, or where
Instead I'll do as you have said
And I will cast my care

In trouble I will run to thee
As David I shall hide
Your shelter is the place for me
When all is wrong outside

And I will rest upon the rock
The pillar for us all
The tower being high and strong
Protector from a fall

I do not thirst, there is no drought
You quench me very well
And when the fire blaze around
The scent I cannot smell

Who is this man? This bread of life
He is the Holy Son
The risen King, my everything
The Bread for everyone.

SOMETIMES

Sometimes my absence will give you your presence.
Sometimes, I think sometimes.

Sometimes my silence will give you your voice.
Assuredly sometimes, I believe sometimes

Sometimes my closure is an open for you.
This door is sometimes, oh yes, sometimes

Sometimes a no from me will help you say yes to you
Praise God sometimes, in fact sometimes

Sometimes these things are the best for you,
Sometimes, so I'll give you your
Sometimes.

EVER

I'm ever so in love with you
My day is not my day
Tomorrow it will cease to be
If you're not here to stay

I love you with a piercing love
It travels through the soul
Forever and eternity
For us it is my goal

I looked into my yester-year
And pondered on my past
How empty was my lonely heart
And then you came at last

A pitter in my beating heart
A patter in my eyes
A smile as wide as east to west
And then to my surprise

You loved me with a Godly love
You held me ever close
You found the hidden side of me
But what I love the most

You lead and yet you give me space
I have my time alone
But lonely is a distant state
My heart has found a home

In you, In you, a love so true
Oh ever it will be
A never ending, lasting love
I have from you to me

THE TEARS OF CHRIST

The tears of Christ are flowing strong
His spirit now is grieved
For every nail and all His blood
And yet He's not believed

The tears of Christ behold the grief
Each time we are in doubt
Each time we try to stand alone
And try to figure out

The woes of life the trials to come
He wants us all to cast
A worry, bother, or concern
In Him it soon will pass

Unyielding trust that He is there
No matter big or small
He wants your faith and all your hope
That He can save from all

A no may be the best for us
Not that He can't comply
The yes may be a time away
If right, He won't deny

So when we dare to hesitate
Reserve within our hearts
Misgivings that He will not show
That's when the crying starts

Hold out in faith believing Him
That all in time is right
And that is how we all can stop
The tears of Jesus Christ

WEIGHT

Up and down then down and up
The pounds they come and go
I gain it fast and faster yet
But losing it is slow

It's liter two then hour glass
A six to twenty-four
Bikini flare and then a glare
I've gained it back and more

I might have had some chocolate chips
That brought about the bulge
And ice cream may have played a part
In truth if I divulge

I sampled sweet potato pies
I gobbled down some cake
That might explain my tummy round
And even belly aches

But Nutrisystem needs a girl
Weight Watchers wants a friend
Slim Fast has a shake for me
My challenge now begins

I'll drink a breakfast in the morn
I'll weigh myself at noon
Then pop a meal into the mic
My food I will consume

With New Year's being very close
I think I'll take the bait
And make a resolution then
To lose a lot of weight

LOVE, LOVE, LOVE

What is this thing? This beating thing
This pounding in my heart
This flutter in my stomach strong
From day into the dark

It has me chasing people down
To tell them that I care
It has me working overtime
To show them I am there

I'm calling, texting, everyday
"It's you I'm thinking of."
It's like a spring, what is this thing?
It's love, it's love, it's love

And then there is a special kind
I've set apart for one
It's like a force I've never felt
Comparison is none

I think about him on a drive
And when I try to eat
He's on my mind, yes, all the time
With him I am complete

For friends I'd do most anything
I'd help, I'd give, and pray,
I think of them and sink or swim
I'd help them everyday

My children have the best of all
My love, my love, my love
Is past by only Christ Himself
My savior up above

A LITTLE PRAYER

It's just a little simple prayer
No problems on my mind
No troubled days that I can see
All worries far behind

A thank you to my Lord above
Awareness of His hands
They cover me and I can see
His love forever stands

I'll put myself on bended knees
I'll close my eyes and pray
I'll think upon the many times
God surely made a way

And then I'll lay upon the floor
I'll gladly contemplate
On all the dangers never seen
Upon Him I shall wait

Oh yes, I've had my nights of tears
But when the morning came
Much joy was springing from my soul
The sun dried up the rain

Therefore, it's only fitting that
I give unto Him praise
Not lifting up my needs and such
I'm in a "THANKING" phase

It's just a simple little prayer
My thoughts go up to you
I only want to thank you for
The many things you do

DEEPEST

Even in my deepest pain
Somehow, I know you're there
And when I'm at the end of ends
You give me strength to bear

For me it is a surgeon's knife
Your source could be of man
A love that left you all alone
A friend who would not stand

No matter of the who or what
Not even when or why
The healing we will only find
When looking to the sky

No tear is wasted that we shed
No hurt unnoticed too
In time to come for all or one
The Lord will see us through

And this is why I press beyond
A pain, a hurt, or wrong
Because the thing to weaken me
Will often make me strong

So cry if crying be at hand
Be silent when you're done
Then listen for the voice that says
"Your victory is won!"

Even in my deepest pain
Fret not is what I hear
For comfort is not far away
In fact, it's very near

MY LOVE

My love is strong for you.

The wind can't blow it, life stresses can't break it,

and there's no fear that can chase me away.

I'm in your life and you in mines because I love you.

My love is truth for you.

There's not a lie that can come and remain,

for my sword of truth will cut it apart

and swipe it into nonexistence because I am your guard

My love is health to you

I'll heal any hurt and cover all your scars with

My bandage of love

I'll pamper even the depth of your soul if you allow me to

My love is strong for you

Truth for you

The very health of you

This is my declaration for

MY LOVE

OOPS

Oops I think I wet my pants
My boobs are on the floor
My memory has gone from me
Each day I'm changing more

My hair is greyer everyday
My sight is growing dim
Once looking like a cover girl
But now I need a gym

How did my youth of yester-year
Just up and run from me
Where is the smoothest, softest skin?
It's wrinkles that I see

"Oh bother," say's my Winnie pooh
But I say bother not
Just think of all the whims and woes
That I have now forgot

Then think about the sleeping in
The rocking in my chair
No clocking in, no crazy boss
Oh peace, you fill my air

And maybe now my teeth are false
My hair is now a wig
My smile is still forever bright
My heart is just as big

It's but a number, growing old
As far as I can see
I'm just as useful, just as loved
I'm happy being me.

IT'S RAINING

It's raining on this weekend day
The clouds are everywhere
But still I feel the warming sun
With plenty heat to share

And birds are hiding in their nests
Yet chirping I do hear
In one accord, and Oh my Lord
It's changed the atmosphere

The sun has stopped the pouring rain
The gray has turned to blue
Another rose has come to be
It's such a precious view

I'll walk along the watered grass
And splash a puddle wide
At least that's what I plan to do
Perhaps when I'm outside

For now I'll think upon the rain
Of how it spoke to me
A symbol that it's washed away
Unpleasant miseries

It also serves as nature's douse
To quench when all is dry
And also as a time to rest
To let the world go by

It's raining on this weekend day
A peaceful, calming, time
The day for now is at a calm
So dear and so sublime

I'M FASHIONED

I'm fashioned in the walk of Christ
I'm mirrored in His ways
At least that is a goal of mines
In Him I'm so amazed

I marvel how He loves me so
As such I want to be
Forgiving, caring, full of grace
A light for all to see

If need I'll turn the other cheek
Look past a state of mind
Not claiming that you are a foe
By chance if you're unkind

I'll strive to heal a hurting heart
An open arm in need
To be a shield to cover you
If hungry, I shall feed

The growth in Christ will bear a sign
A sign that I'm mature
Although it may be hard at times
All things I shall endure

In hopes to be a beacon bright
A bridge that you may cross
I pray to be a waving flag
To signal all who's lost

I'm fashioned in the way of Christ
True Christians are the same
We're here to lead you to Lord
It's done in Jesus name

IF GOOD

If good, I'll keep it close to me
If bad, I'll let it go
A love, a friend, through thick and thin
If not, then this is so

I'll love you from a distance far
I'll pray the best for you
And should we be a world apart
Then this is what I'll do

I'll send a letter through the mail
Like that of olden times
Your needs I'll lift them up to God
As if the needs were mines

And who's to say in time to come
That we won't meet again
Forgiveness is the building bridge
To keep us close as friends

If words were said without a thought
I'll clear them from my head
Sometimes we slip, sometimes we fall
So what I'll do instead

I'll cover with the love of Christ
For this is what I'm taught
For love is grand, and it will stand
By chance if there's a fault

If good, I'll keep it close to me
If bad, then I will pray
That God will use it as a tool
To bring you back my way

LOVE FOR YOU

The highest mountain is as a molehill compared to my **love for you**.

Truly the depth of an ocean is a puddle equated to my **love for you**. If it's distance, I'm

wider, strength, I'm stronger and weakness is as none when resting in my **love for you**. If

your heart yearns for something higher, it will be found in God, for only He loves you more

than I. There's no jealousy in this truth and you can rest with assurance, for it is He who gives

me instructions on how to daily show

my **love for you.**

EVEN

Even when I'm at my worst
That ugly, hidden, side
The world beholds my Jekyll's best
But you see Mrs. Hyde

And even when I fake a smile
You see my inner frown
On lookers see me right side up
You know I've fallen down

But that is why I love you so
You know my deepest thought
The lashings that I keep within
The battles that I've fought

You cover that it's never known
I'm cradled in your arms
Then I can slumber into sleep
And oh, your precious charm

You love me with the purest love
So meek and strong alike
And when the world has weakened me
You're there to take the fight

Though Jesus left His Spirit man
To live inside of me
He's way up high and yet in you
In you His face I see

So even when I'm at my worst
Your love is as a shore
You flood me with your very best
You love me to the core

MIND

I'm searching for a brilliant mind
I'm empty as can be
No thoughts, or dust, nor anything
My head is clutter free

I thought it to be fun at first
No problems to behold
But then I thought of memories
The ones from days of old

I can't recite a nursery rhyme
In fact I can't recall
My day of birth, my middle name
My mind has lost it all

And so I'm asking for a trade
A mind so full of zeal
A mind to reason everything
Like how to cook a meal

A mind to drive me to the store
Then get me back again
A mind to call my children's name
At least a special friend

Now lonely thoughts or hurting thoughts
You stay among the loss
But if I've won the lottery
Then gladly come across

This mind of old, but still of gold
The one thing that I know
The thought of love fits as a glove
And never will it go

IF I COULD CHANGE

If I could change the hands of time
And move them back to youth
I doubt that I would change a lot
And that's the simple truth

I still would long to be a wife
A mother full of glee
I'd serve the Lord with all my heart
And write my poetry

I'd friend the strangers in a world
At times so full of hate
I'd act as if they're family
I would not hesitate

In looking back I'm pretty sure
Decisions that I made
Perfect no, but right for me
Therefore, I would not trade

The Lord He has a special way
From bad He brings the good
And so I do not wish for change
Not even if I could

Oh maybe I would watch my weight
At first instead of last
But only for the gain of health
While looking in my past

If I could change the hands of time
This hope so very true
I'd hold a loved one once again
And tell them, "I love you."

HUMBLED

I'm humbled to the end of me
So willing to bow down
And eager to be out of sight
No people to be found

I'll gladly take the last of seats
Where I cannot be seen
Sometimes it's good to be alone
To listen to the King

In Him I find the strength to heal
Not chained unto my past
Sometimes a hurt will come to be
But I who make it last

I've tried to be the judge of judge
Not willing to forgive
Yet I alone was in a cell
In prison I did live

But who am I to see a speck
A splinter in an eye
Then over look the plank in me
That reaches to the sky

I'd rather focus on the one
The righter of all wrong
In youth mistakes are often made
But change can come along

So I will humble all of me
Forgive to past the test
In this I know that I have grown
For all I pray the best

IT'S YOURS

In my insolence, ignorance, and pride I tried to carry my burdens.

Now I've concluded that I can't, and I humbly say, IT'S YOURS.

Education was my crutch, societal position, my high; sadly, titles were my claim to illusional fame, and as Solomon said, "It's vanity", therefore, these falsities I now say, IT'S YOURS.

My heart, IT'S YOURS, commitment, diligence, faithfulness, IT'S YOURS. Even my silent cries, fears, hurts, and my tears, at last my God, IT'S YOURS.

Gladly with peace and serenity today my life, IT'S YOURS.

MEMORY

My photographic memory
Has packed its final thought
So empty is my open mind
It all has come to naught

So lonely are the spider webs
That's filling every space
Knowledge, wisdom truths and facts
They all have been replaced

But I am not in mourning for
I now can strive to be
The person that I've dreamed about
That kid inside of me

I might become the unicorn
They say that never was
A human elf, or Santa Claus
A heart of endless love

I might become a peeping Tom
To look into your soul
Then find a way to bring about
Your deepest, inner goals

So worries take your needed leave
Forgetful now I am
I don't remember hurtful things
And happy I do stand

My photographic memory
Does hold a picture clear
My love for you, my need of you
My friend so very dear

GENTLE

A gentle push I have for you
Perhaps a little shove
But know the things I tend to do
I do it so in love

The slightest pull when holding you
A squeeze upon your hand
And if I am confusing you
Please try and understand

I see a greatness deep within
A giant standing tall
I see a strength you do behold
That's needed for us all

I see a passion burning bright
A light you do not see
Illumination for the world
And that's including me

So loving are the ways of you
So caring is your touch
So needed are the traits in you
I mean this very much

The pulling that you surely feel
I hope is showing you
There is job awaiting now
That only you can do

I have a gentle, little shove
A leading to a goal
And now I gladly step aside
So you can take control

HIS GRACE

His grace is more than filling me
In presence of my soul
His grace is there to strengthen me
In things I can't control

A challenge long or mountain high
In Him I can sustain
Not fretting what I'm going through
Therefore, I won't complain

When I am faced with troubled times
On Him I keep my sight
I gather hope I witness peace
When God is my delight

I've learned to be of stable mind
If walking through a storm
I've learned to trust and more believe
God gives beyond the norm

So there may be a night or two
Of want perhaps a need
But faith is strong because I know
He will supply indeed

Abase are times I've had before
Abound I've had the more
For grace has always been with me
But this I can't ignore

If I am at the height of life
Or trouble face to face
I know that I can handle all
Because I have His grace

THERE ARE MOMENTS

There are moments I'm about my day, but then there's a sight, a
fragrance, or music, and it hits me that you're gone.
There are moments, oh there are moments.

I'm working, I'm laughing, I'm doing me, but then there's a picture, a
memory, a reminder that you left me.
There are moments, yes there are moments.

A bracelet you gave me, advice that saved me, the warmest of blankets
that encased me, but it's not you.
There are moments, God there are moments.

Yet the hope that I have is your peace and at last
No sickness to bind or to hurt you.
That's a good moment, in fact, a great moment.

'Till I see my loved ones again

A WHISPER

A whisper from the blowing wind
It's from my lover true
A secret carried in the breeze
Oh what am I to do?

I cannot keep it close to me
It's passing far away
Not giving me the chance to speak
Come back that I may say

I thank you for the loving words
That blew into my ear
And if the wind returns to me
I'll make it crystal clear

I love you with the purest heart
So rarely do I show
The deepest and the center part
Of me for one to know

But I have given all of me
To you until the end
My love of loves, but most of all
You are my closest friend

Yet if a bird is close to me
I'll send a message back
A secret sealed with kisses true
And know that it's a fact

The whispers in the coming wind
Will Wrap around you close
And say to you that it is true
I love you so the most

IT'S HARD

It's hard for me to work today
The sun is shining bright
My inner child is going wild
So I must do it right

I simply can't adult today
I won't be paying bills
I won't be eating balanced food
It's cookies every meal

Oh never mind the belly ache
The rotting of my teeth
I'll think about the consequence
For now I'll take a leap

The wading pool or swimming pool
The size is not a thought
The office is a problem now
But ever if I'm caught

I'll tell the boss to take a hike
I'll give the crew a raise
We'll party in the conference room
Then after many days

We'll play a game I really love
It's tag and you are it
And if the board won't go along
Then all of us will quit

It's hard for me to work today
The moon is on the rise
So I will watch the brightest star
Across the friendly skies

DO YOU SUPPOSE

Do you suppose when seasons go
They struggle hard to leave?
Upon return is there a yearn
To be what they can't be?

Will summer snow and winter shine?
Will fall hold back her wind?
Will spring refuse to bring her bloom?
To never be again?

If this is no then tell me so
Why do we try to be?
The likes of him, the ways of her
Why do we fail to see?

We are unique and set apart
All special in our way
No greater than no lesser than
But better day by day

Voluptuous within a shape
Be tall or very short
Or long in hair with skin so fair
We come in many sorts

The crayons have variety
Vast colors they behold
A master piece when they are used
A story to be told

Do you suppose that we can be
Crayola side by side
Blending, sharing, standing close
With love and full of pride

BEHIND THE DOORS

Behind the doors beyond the view
Where no one else can see
There is a praise from deep within
A praise to you from me

Out of the sight of everyone
Who do not see my tears
Who do not know my troubled heart
Who do not know my fears

I open up to you oh Lord
I share my inner thoughts
I tell what others cannot know
I share what I have lost

But in the sharing through my pain
Within me there is peace
And then I shout and dance alone
For you do bare my grief

A spirit praise, an honest praise
A praise so pure and true
I do not dance for man to see
It's private and for you

It's not that I'm afraid to show
The world my holy dance
Some views are just for you the see
But when I have the chance

I'll tell the masses everything
I'll tell them all of you
For now I'll stay beyond the doors
This is a private view

I KNOW IT'S HARD

I know it's hard; new challenges often are.

I know it's frightening; the unknown can bring about fear.

I know it's frustrating; new beginnings have a habit of being that way.

I know you're at your wit's end, but your end is God's beginning.

I KNOW

COLOR BLIND

Let me speak my inner truth
The fact that's on my mind
I'm thanking God and praising God
That I am color blind

I do not see your shade of skin
Not black, not white, nor gold
Your status will not catch my eye
My heart I must unfold

I see the fighting back and forth
The judging of a race
The hating dark, or hating light
I do not have the space

We're unaware when we are born
Of gender this is true
And pigmentation is unknown
So this is what I do

I look into the inner man
I dare to see the heart
I'm searching with the eyes of love
And if you do your part

We'll have a world so full of peace
We'd love beyond the skin
We'd gather close and hand and hand
The loving can begin

We'd have a love forever true
A Godly heart and mind
So join me that the world may be
A world that's color blind

BEFORE

Before the overflow from God
There may be times of lack
Then just enough, but sure enough
God always has your back

And though abundance is to come
Some bills fall overdue
While healing is a dream away
So what are we to do?

These are the times of using faith
A walking beyond sight
A knowing when you do not see
That God will make it right

It is a time of living life
Without a troubled heart
And trusting when the time is right
That God will do His part

A no for now, perhaps for good
Still count it as a win
Delayed, denied, endure the ride
The best is at the end

Do rest assured your overflow
Abundance even more
Is on the way and every hope
Is well worth waiting for

ALL I KNOW

All I know is press and pray
This thing, it too, shall pass
Some nights are long and full of wrong
In truth, they will not last

And all I know is stand my ground
To wait and know that He
Is on the thrown and it is known
All things that trouble me

It's true some problems come to light
To darken all my hope
But that is when I doubled down
My faith does help me cope

For roses cannot come to be
Lest rain falls from the sky
To moisten dirt that covers them
And so, no questions, why

I know that eagles drop their young
And though the act is cruel
It's then the eaglets learn to fly
Their feathers strong and full

Therefore, I see the stressful times
As lessons to be learned
Of how to trust and how to wait
Remaining calm and stern

So all I know is press and pray
His timing's always right
They may begin, but trouble ends
Henceforth, a peaceful night

A COVERED SOUL

A covered soul with poetry
For sure it was my goal
A rhyming force to cradle you
With poems for the Soul

I wanted so to penetrate
The private, inner side
Where people cannot enter in
The place you go to hide

I pray I opened up for you
A world of inner peace
A space to calm a racing mind
Where fear can be released

I pray I made you laugh aloud
With tears upon your cheek
I pray you found your greatest strength
That you're no longer weak

Perhaps you fell in love again
Increased your walk with Christ
A line or two that changed a view
A wrong turned into right

If I have blessed with rhyming words
From start until the end
I'm ever grateful through and through
For now I rest my pen

The book is Poems for the Soul
Like Jesus covered blood
I pray I wrapped you with my rhymes
That's covered so in love

Greeting Card Intro

It is a privilege and an honor to feature on the last pages of "Poems for the Soul", poems from my up and coming greeting card line. These are greeting cards for all occasions including holidays, birthdays, graduation, and sympathy.

All though I've been writing greeting cards for a while now, this will be the first time they'll be boxed and ready for order. Much like my poetry books, they will make you laugh, cry, think, comfort, and encourage. Unlike my calendars though, theses greeting cards will be available in duplications, so that you can mail out your favorite card to everyone on you mailing list.

All work is original, new, and as always, Godly inspired. I look forward to serving you in yet another poetic venture and so, please enjoy the intro to my greeting card line.

SAVE A SPOT

Just in case I cannot sit
Beneath your Christmas tree
Wrap a box with pretty bows
To save a spot for me

And just in case the packages
I sent from me to you
Are late do look inside your heart
And know this to be true

I'm sending out my very best
A Merry Christmas cheer
With wishes that your dream of dreams
Will gather to you near

I pray for wealth and health for you
But most of all the goal
Is that you have an inner peace
To rest within your soul

If weather sends a heavy snow
And roads I cannot pass
Then reminisce on times of bliss
And have a hearty laugh

Deck the halls and jingle bells
Those awesome Christmas songs
Tell me that the time is close
I know it won't be long

I'll ring your bell and enter in
For real or fantasy
In your house or in your heart
Please save a spot for me

ANOTHER YEAR

Another year has come around
A birthday for my dad
A grateful year of glee and cheer
You're still a youthful lad

I hope you have the biggest cake
The sweetest in the land
With boxes filled with everything
And more than you can stand

I better plan for everyone
To gather at your side
To sing of love, of peace, and joy
With arms spread open wide

We'll pull you near unto our hearts
Give kisses on your cheek
We'll make you laugh a hearty laugh
Until your legs are weak

And being that I'm very spoiled
I'll sit upon your knee
Not letting others share the space
That's set aside for me

True older yes and better still
I pray that life has been
The biggest, brightest, greatest thing
On this you can depend

I wish you well as you can tell
When reading every line
And may today and everyday
Be blessed and very kind

GRADUATION DAY

I knew the day that you were born
Before you crawled or talked
The day at hand from babe to man
Across the stage you walk

I knew before you bounced a ball
And tossed it in the air
That in return an honor earned
And surely I'd be there

So now the future's come to be
And what more can I say
I'm grateful that I'm here to see
Your graduation day

A giant as you glide across
The stage of brighten lights
Unveiling how you studied hard
For long and endless nights

And now the torch is given you
The proof of knowledge, vast
For every test that came your way
With grace, you truly passed

I'm proud is such a simple phrase
And happy can't begin
To show, express, convey, confess
I hope it never ends

The quest to learn all that you can
Let nothing block your way
Hugs so true, congrats to you
Enjoy this special day

IT TOOK A WHILE

It took a while to take a pen
And write these words so true
Today, today, you went away
And I am missing you

The flesh, the flesh, this selfish flesh
Just won't accept the fact
You are released your soul at peace
Therefore you won't be back

But rather cry a mourning cry
I choose to be in praise
And when the tears roll down my face
My head I'll surely raise

Then look unto the hills above
Because it holds my help
True God alone has seen it all
This loss, I know, He's felt

And then I'll think how free you are
No illness in your way
No sadness to bewilder you
And to the Lord I say

I thank you for a promise kept
No sorrows when we leave
No weight to clutter up our minds
To this I wholly cleave

That I will see you once again
No guess and not by chance
I'll see the Angels be in awe
As they behold your dance

Thank You

www.ingramcontent.com/pod-product-compliance
Lightning Source LLC
Chambersburg PA
CBHW071416290426
44108CB00014B/1843